*sparkteach

TEACHING THE CLASSICS TO TODAY'S STUDENTS

1984

GEORGE ORWELL

*sparkteach

ISBN 978-1-4114-7993-7

Distributed in Canada by Sterling Publishing Co., Inc.
c/o Canadian Manda Group, 664 Annette Street
Toronto, Ontario M6S 2C8, Canada
Distributed in the United Kingdom by GMC Distribution Services
Castle Place, 166 High Street, Lewes, East Sussex BN7 1XU, England
Distributed in Australia by NewSouth Books
University of New South Wales, Sydney, NSW 2052, Australia

For information about custom editions, special sales, and premium
and corporate purchases, please contact Sterling Special Sales
at 800-805-5489 or specialsales@sterlingpublishing.com.

Manufactured in Canada

2 4 6 8 10 9 7 5 3 1

sparkteach.com
sparknotes.com
sterlingpublishing.com

Cover design by Elizabeth Mihaltse Lindy
Cover and title page illustration by MUTI
Interior design by Kevin Ullrich and Christine Heun
Image credits: iStock/Getty Images Plus: filborg: 14, 15; Shutterstock.com:
Everett Collection: 24; KarSol: 25; Tela: 23 bottom; Znakki: 23 top

Contents

PART 1

Welcome to SparkTeach!

SparkTeach is a unique set of teaching guides and lesson plans designed to help make classic literature engaging and relevant to today's students.

We asked teachers about the biggest challenges they face in their English classes, and their answer was clear: "We need to engage our students, spark their interest in literature, and make our lessons relevant." That's why we developed SparkTeach, customizable materials including teaching frameworks, lessons, in-class worksheets, and more for the most popular titles taught today!

The following pages provide you with helpful tips for lesson planning and classroom management, an explanation of each component, including a detailed description of a "Real-Life Lens Lesson"; an explanation of the role of the ELA Common Core State Standards in the program; and guidelines for student assessment.

SparkTeach materials are easily customizable and can be adapted for many different learning styles. We encourage you to utilize the lessons as best fits your classroom's needs.

Tips for Class Planning and Management

Here are some tips for planning and managing your class as students work their way through a SparkTeach unit. To maximize student learning and engagement:

1. Preview SparkTeach Materials

Review all the materials available for a text. Decide which worksheets you will use based on student needs. You may choose materials to match a particular text in your curriculum, or you may assign a text after being inspired by a specific Real-Life Lens Lesson.

2. Gather Your Materials

Once you've selected the components you'll need, preview each lesson and then reproduce all of the chosen worksheets. Be sure to reproduce enough copies for each student and one copy for yourself to use as reference. Hand out all worksheets needed prior to reading, such as Contextual Support Handouts, as these promote student comprehension.

Review the Midpoint Activities and Final Project options in the Real-Life Lens Lesson. Will you need specific equipment such as a video recorder or a printer for students to complete a project? Be sure your students will have access to the tools they'll need to complete their work.

3. Set Your Schedule

Once you've chosen a Real-Life Lens Lesson, read it through before starting. Choose your start, midpoint, and end dates to keep on schedule. Each framework should take multiple class periods to complete; plan each activity and project accordingly. Will students need access to the school library or the internet to conduct research for their final projects? If so, be sure to schedule time for student research, review, and revision.

4. Preview Real-Life Links

Read, watch, or listen to each of the Real-Life Links. Decide which resources will engage your students the most. Prepare a few questions to use to ignite student thinking, guide quick written responses, and initiate class discussion.

5. Monitor Student Progress and Comprehension

Routinely schedule one-on-one meetings with students to check their comprehension and progress throughout reading. During group work or discussions, circulate around the room to monitor student collaboration and communication and to gently guide discussions back on topic, if necessary. Recording your observations and assessments will enable you to note individual and whole-class progress as work continues.

6. Let Students Shine

Schedule plenty of time for all students to present their final projects. They have worked hard all month, and showing off their finished work boosts confidence and allows students to see the unique and creative ways their peers interpreted and approached a similar topic.

7. Personalize Content

Real-Life Lens Lessons are designed to ensure students engage with each text in a meaningful way. Lenses are specially chosen to help students connect with even the most challenging texts on a personal level. As you progress through the materials, look for ways to help students relate the text to their own lives. Notice what excites them and tailor your lessons accordingly.

What's Included in SparkTeach?

Real-Life Lens Lessons

The Real-Life Lens Lesson is a unit that focuses on a specific text over multiple class periods. The driving force behind each unit is the lens, a carefully selected theme through which students view the text. This lens provides students with a relatable point of entry. A thorough explanation of each feature in a Real-Life Lens Lesson is detailed in the next section beginning on page 8. Each Real-Life Lens Lesson includes several reproducible worksheets and assessment materials to round out the unit.

Reading Skills Worksheets

Each set of teaching materials features multiple Reading Skills Worksheets designed to help develop the ELA reading skills outlined in the Common Core State Standards. Worksheets engage students in a variety of activities that deepen understanding of both the skill and the featured text. Each worksheet is reproducible.

Vocabulary Builders

Each set of teaching materials also includes at least one Vocabulary Builder based on the specific language found in the text. You can pass out the builder prior to starting the text and refer to it as students read to ensure comprehension. Other builders ask students to engage with the vocabulary through graphic organizers, charts, or other activities. Each builder is reproducible.

Contextual Support Handouts

To aid comprehension, each set of teaching materials features at least one Contextual Support handout to provide information to students about topics relevant to the text. Student comprehension is hindered if historical or background information is unknown or not clear. We developed these handouts to arm students with the information they'll need to better understand each text.

Comprehension Check Quizzes

Check your students' comprehension of the text and understanding of various plot elements and characters with the 25-question Full Book Quiz and 5-question Section Quizzes. These quizzes are reproducible and come with answer keys.

What Makes Real-Life Lens Lessons Unique?

Real-Life Lens Lessons, the hub of SparkTeach materials, set this literature program apart. Each Real-Life Lens Lesson is thoughtfully designed to help students view the text—even older or more challenging works—through a relatable lens that enables students to connect with the text in a meaningful way. A powerful teaching tool, each teacher-facing Real-Life Lens Lesson provides a framework for organizing and executing a unit over multiple class periods that focuses on a particular work of literature. Each element found in a Real-Life Lens Lesson is listed and described below.

1. The Lens

The lens is the heart of each Real-Life Lens Lesson. The lens shapes classroom discussions, student analysis, and all lesson activities and projects. The lens invites students to explore the text in a way that connects the content with their own lives—their experiences, concerns, interests, and aspirations.

Introduce the Lens Through Real-Life Links

- Each Real-Life Lens Lesson features several Real-Life Links including online articles, podcasts, videos, and surveys.

- Real-Life Links are meant to be shared with students prior to or during reading.

- After students read, listen to, or watch the Real-Life Links, but before reading of the text begins, the class participates in an activity designed to introduce the lens to students in a meaningful way.

2. Big Idea Questions

- The Big Idea Questions are overarching questions that provide students with a base from which to start thinking about the text. For example: "How does language provide freedom?" (See page 15.)

- Students are encouraged to return to these questions as they read and note how their answers to the questions change over the course of the unit.

3. Driving Questions

In addition to the Big Idea Questions, each Real-Life Lens Lesson contains a number of Driving Questions. Unlike the Big Idea Questions, Driving Questions are more specific in their focus and are designed to guide student exploration of the text, as related to the lens. Some examples of Driving Questions featured in *1984* include:

- What changes with each new edition of the Newspeak dictionary?

- How is Newspeak different from Oldspeak?

- What is the significance of calling Oceania's ruler "Big Brother"?

4. Differentiated Instruction

- To ensure all students can access learning, we have provided differentiated instruction for all Midpoint Activities and final projects.

- Suggestions for increasing and/or decreasing the difficulty of each activity and project are found throughout each Real-Life Lens Lesson.

5. Midpoint Activities

- Two engaging Midpoint Activities are featured to ensure student comprehension of the text and give you an opportunity to assess learning.

- These activities encourage students to consolidate their understanding of the text so far and challenge them to use that understanding to make predictions about the rest of the text and analyze what they know of the plot, characters, or theme.

6. Paired Text Recommendations

- Our list of paired text recommendations suggests contemporary works you can pair with the classic work you're teaching.

- Students can connect to passages from multiple works by comparing, contrasting, and analyzing the works side by side.

7. Final Projects

- Each Real-Life Lens Lesson presents students with two options for final projects that encapsulate what they have learned about the text as seen through the lens.

- Students are invited to choose the project that excites them the most at the beginning of the unit and to keep this project in mind as they read.

- These dynamic projects are designed to provide opportunities for students to demonstrate their mastery of the text in creative and fun ways.

- Examples of projects include creating a multimedia presentation or video, rewriting and performing a scene from the text, and participating in a formal debate on a specific issue.

8. Supporting Worksheets and Graphic Organizers

- Each Real-Life Lens Lesson offers several reproducible worksheets, including a **Driving Questions Worksheet, located on page 38,** on which students can record answers as they read, and graphic organizers to support student learning.

- To save you time and help students understand how to tackle each task, each worksheet includes scaffolded directions and a sample student response if necessary.

9. Student and Teacher Reflection Worksheets

- The **Student Reflection Worksheet, located on page 70,** encourages students to assess their strengths, weaknesses, and level of engagement throughout the Real-Life Lens Lesson.

- Self-assessment cultivates confidence, as students note how they worked through challenges; nurtures good study habits; and encourages students to take responsibility for their own learning.

- The **Teacher Reflection Worksheet, located on page 71,** allows you to evaluate what elements of the unit students found the most engaging, where they seemed to struggle, and what approaches or elements worked the best for you and your class.

SparkTeach and the Common Core State Standards

Every component included in SparkTeach was developed to ensure broad coverage of the ELA Common Core State Standards. Materials were designed to provide multiple opportunities for your students to address a wide variety of Reading Literature, Speaking and Listening, Writing, and Language standards.

   Each standard addressed by an activity, discussion, or project is listed for easy reference so that you can track which standards each lesson or worksheet covers.

Guidelines for Student Assessment

Each set of SparkTeach materials provides extensive assessment opportunities, including a **Rubric for Student Assessment, a Student Reflection Worksheet, and a Teacher Reflection Worksheet (see pages 66–71)**. Use these assets, along with lesson-specific assessment advice within each Real-Life Lens Lesson, to successfully gauge student learning.

Worksheet Assessment

Many Reading Skills Worksheets and Vocabulary Builders may be scored in a traditional fashion. To make grading easier and faster, we have provided full answer keys for worksheets that contain clear correct or incorrect answers and sample student answers for worksheets that require more subjective, open-ended answers.

Real-Life Lens Lesson Assessment

Each Real-Life Lens Lesson offers opportunities for informal, formal, and self-assessment. Performance assessment involves observing student collaboration, while formal assessment entails grading a writing assignment, worksheet, or final project.

PART 2

SparkTeach
1984
Lesson Plan

Real-Life Lens Lesson *1984*

Language as a Form of Control

Use this Real-Life Lens Lesson to help students dive deep into George Orwell's *1984* and examine the novel's themes, action, and characters through the lens of language as a form of control. How do the Party leaders use Newspeak to influence how people think and feel? Is their manipulation effective? What are the dangers when it comes to controlling people through the words they use?

Materials

1984 by George Orwell

Worksheets: Driving Questions, page 38

Shades of Meaning, page 41

Introduce the Lens

To activate students' thinking, choose one or two of the following Real-Life Links to use in an engagement activity. Have students read or listen and discuss the content. Encourage students to jot down notes, or record class notes on the board for future reference.

Real-Life Links: The Power in Language

Controlling People Through Language

This article from the Transnational Institute explores ways that different cultures use language to respond to and shape the values of their society.

https://rb.gy/eemljo

From the Power of Language to the Language of Power

In this TEDx Talk, neurologist Peter Garrard explains how power and language influence each other.

https://rb.gy/ds30sg

How the Media Uses Language to Manipulate You

This article by Kristina Adams explains how the media uses specific language to reach an audience as well as how that language varies by culture.

https://rb.gy/4qi0vp

How Language Shapes the Way We Think

In this TED Talk, cognitive scientist Lera Boroditsky explores how different languages shape the values and thoughts of the people who speak them.

https://rb.gy/fedoj4

Pose the Following Big Idea Questions to the Class:

How does language provide freedom?

How do the words we use shape our thoughts?

Engagement Activity

Have students write quick initial responses to the questions. Then discuss the questions either as a class or in small groups. Prompt students to consider the relationship between language and thoughts. Encourage students to think about how the words they use allow them to have a range of beliefs about certain subjects. Following discussion, give students time to revise their initial responses, and ask volunteers to share what they wrote with the class.

CCSS: SL.11-12.1

Introduce the Driving Questions

Begin by having students write their own questions about the lesson topic. Encourage them to think about what they already know about language as a form of control and what they're interested in exploring further.

Hand out the **Driving Questions Worksheet, located on page 38**. Review the questions as a class. Students should enter initial answers to the questions before and as they read *1984*. They will revisit the questions and revise their answers following the lesson activities, classroom discussion, and the completion of the text. Remind students to support their responses with text evidence.

Integrate the Driving Questions into your classroom discussions. Use them to help guide students' thinking about the Big Idea Questions.

1. How is Newspeak different from Oldspeak?
2. What changes with each new edition of the Newspeak dictionary?
3. What is the purpose in developing Newspeak?
4. How does Newspeak limit people's freedom?
5. What is the significance of calling Oceania's ruler "Big Brother"?
6. What contradictions exist in Newspeak?
7. Why can't citizens of Oceania learn other languages?
8. How does the Party use Newspeak to control people's feelings and emotions?

CCSS: RL.11-12.1, W.11-12.4

Introduce the "Through the Lens" Activity

Activity 1: Personal Experience with Language

In this activity, students will write about how learning a new language can benefit people.

Ask students to write a paragraph about how learning new languages can benefit people. In their paragraphs, students may describe the freedoms that come with learning new languages, such as being able to communicate with others in foreign countries, understanding the origins of words or phrases in their own language, and learning words with specific meanings that do not exist in their own language.

Pair students and have partners share their paragraphs. Encourage pairs to return to the Big Idea Questions and consider how their background knowledge informed their initial answers.

Invite three or four students to share their paragraphs with the class. Prompt whole-class discussion with questions such as the following: *Have you ever visited a foreign country and been unable to communicate with others? If you have learned a second language, did it teach you more about your native language? Have you ever learned a word in a foreign language that expresses something that your native language does not express as succinctly? Do members of your family speak different languages or dialects than you?*

Before moving on, explain that students will explore Orwell's treatment of language as a form of control and how he suggests that having access to an expansive language can provide freedom as they read *1984*.

CCSS: SL.11-12.1, W.11-12.3

Differentiated Instruction

This activity can be modified to help all students access learning.

Decrease Difficulty

Suggest ideas for the paragraph, such as being able to ask for directions in a foreign country. Proceed with discussion as outlined above.

Increase Difficulty

Have students write short personal essays about their own experiences with how learning a new language has benefited them or how not knowing a certain language has been prohibitive. Ask two or three students to read their essays to the class and proceed with discussion as outlined above.

Introduce the Final Project

Before moving on, introduce the final projects to the class (see page 19 for details). Have students choose the project they will complete and encourage them to keep their project in mind as they read the text. Facilitate the formation of project groups if necessary.

Assign the Midpoint Activities

Activity 1: Theme: Control

Students will make inferences about how language can be changed to control people's thoughts. Students will work in pairs to identify words that are used in the book that Inner Party members might eliminate from Newspeak to prevent people from committing thought crimes. Have each pair make a list and write notes about each term they choose.

Have students share the words they chose and discuss as a class how the mere existence of certain words and phrases can provide people with freedom and individual thought.

CCSS: RL.11-12.1, SL.11-12.1, W.11-12.2

Differentiated Instruction

Decrease Difficulty

Provide students with examples of words that the author explicitly says do not exist in Newspeak, such as science or individualism. Ask students how not having a word to express these concepts controls not only what people say but also how they think.

Increase Difficulty

Have students write essays explaining how the elimination of certain words and concepts is a key method for the Party to retain control of how people think and therefore act. Be sure students support their arguments with textual evidence.

Activity 2: Shades of Meaning

Students will use the **Shades of Meaning Worksheet, located on page 41**, to explore why having several words that are similar in meaning but have very slight differences is important. Students will work in pairs or groups to:

- list synonyms and antonyms for specific words from *1984*. They can use dictionaries or online resources to help as you prefer.

- explain how having a variety of words with shades of meaning allows people the freedom to express themselves.

Differentiated Instruction

Decrease Difficulty

Scaffold the activity by providing examples of synonyms and antonyms of the words provided. Discuss with them when and why they might use these different words to express specific thoughts.

Increase Difficulty

Have students invent five new Newspeak words. Ask students to define each new word and then use each in a sentence or paragraph.

CCSS: L.11-12.5

Final Projects

Students will work on their final projects after they have finished reading the complete text of *1984*. Project 1 can be completed by students working in groups, while Project 2 can be done individually.

Final Project 1: Propaganda

Students will create multimedia pieces of propaganda to promote a cause. Students will:

- choose a cause to promote, such as an event or issue in the school or community.

- work in small groups to create a multimedia piece of propaganda, such as a video, a poster accompanied by a recorded speech, or a slide show with audio. Tell students to think very carefully about the words they use and which will best persuade people to agree with them.

- present their piece of propaganda to the class and explain as a group why they chose specific words and the effect they intended their language to have on the audience.

- discuss as a class whether or not the language used in the propaganda produced its intended effect.

- write a short follow-up essay describing how the ideas and examples of language as a form of control in *1984* influenced their propaganda project.

CCSS: W.11-12.1, W.11-12.4, W.11-12.6, L.11-12.5, SL.11-12.4

Differentiated Instruction

Decrease Difficulty

Scaffold the project by first providing students with examples of propaganda-based advertisements. Have them discuss how the words used in the advertisements effectively persuade people (or don't).

Increase Difficulty

Inform groups that their propaganda must include visual, audio, and written elements to ensure a wider coverage of the viewer's senses. For an additional challenge, require students to complete this project independently.

Final Project 2: Translate

Students will translate a passage from the Declaration of Independence into Newspeak to explore how Newspeak can eliminate the concept of freedom. Students will:

- read the excerpt from the Declaration of Independence beginning with "We hold these truths to be self-evident" through "and to institute the new Government. . . ."

- translate each word in the excerpt into Newspeak based on what they learned about Newspeak while reading *1984*.

- write a short essay explaining how the meaning of the excerpt changes once translated into Newspeak.

CCSS: W.11-12.1, W.11-12.4

Differentiated Instruction

Decrease Difficulty

Have students translate the passage in pairs before writing their essays individually.

Increase Difficulty

Have students write an original passage based on the structure of the Declaration of Independence but using as much Newspeak as possible. Invite students to share their work with a partner and consider how they each utilized individual words from Newspeak.

Assess the Assignments

Use the **Rubric for Student Assessment, located on page 67,** to evaluate student work on the lesson assignments.

Distribute the **Student Reflection Worksheet, located on page 70**. Guide students through the self-assessment and reflection questions.

Complete the **Teacher Reflection Worksheet, located on page 71**. Record which elements of the lesson plan worked well for your class and which elements you might revise for future classes.

PART 3

Worksheets and Handouts

Totalitarianism, Fascism, and Nazism

Overview

George Orwell understood the dangers posed by the rise of totalitarian governments, and he wrote the novel *1984* as a warning to the world. This handout will provide students with historical information critical to understanding the plot and themes presented in *1984*. Topics such as totalitarianism in the Soviet Union, Nazism in Germany, and dictatorship in Spain are explored. Pass out this support to students prior to reading *1984*. Allow time for discussion and debate in your classroom on the subjects covered.

Totalitarianism, Fascism, and Nazism

Orwell's Warning

George Orwell was inspired to write *1984* as he watched the rise of totalitarian governments across Europe. A totalitarian government provides no individual freedoms and subjects all citizens to the state's authority. It is run by a dictator, who has complete control and who usually came to power by force rather than by the will of the people. Fascism is a type of totalitarianism and is characterized by excessive nationalism, which is a devotion to one's own country even if that devotion is at the expense of other countries.

Totalitarianism in the Soviet Union

The Soviet Union was the first country to be controlled by a totalitarian government after World War I under dictator Joseph Stalin. The Soviet Union was established in 1922 by Vladimir Lenin, who founded the Russian Communist Party. Lenin's goal was for the government to be controlled by the working class. However, after Lenin's death in 1924, Stalin seized control of the Soviet Union and became its dictator. Stalin's government controlled people by using terror, making it known that anyone who opposed him could be murdered at any time. He had a secret police force and encouraged citizens to spy on one another. Before the outbreak of World War II, Stalin and Hitler signed a nonaggression pact, which Germany broke in 1941 by invading the Soviet Union. Stalin's army eventually drove the Germans out of the Soviet Union. Even after World War II, Stalin continued to eliminate any potential opponents by killing them or removing them to forced labor camps. Despite the government's claim that life was better for its citizens under Stalin, most people lived in harsh conditions with food shortages and limited housing. Stalin died in 1953, but the Soviet Union and its totalitarian government were not dissolved until 1991.

Nazi Germany

The Nazi Party, or National Socialist German Workers' Party, was founded in 1919 on the beliefs of nationalism and anti-Semitism. Adolf Hitler became its leader in 1921. Early members of the party were angry about Germany's defeat in World War I and the fact that their economy was suffering as a result. Hitler used Jewish people, along with other groups such as gypsies, Communists, and the disabled, as scapegoats for the problems Germany was facing. He was a charismatic speaker, so his speeches claiming that Germany's problems would be solved by removing anyone who was not part of the "master" race from the country were effective. In 1933, Hitler was appointed chancellor of Germany's government, and Nazi rule began. He banned all political parties except for Nazism and opened what would be the first concentration camp in Dachau. Over the years, Jewish people were banned from most public places. As the government began to arrest people and send them to concentration camps, people began fleeing the country or going into hiding. Hitler called the eventual planned murder of all Jewish people "the final solution." In 1939, Germany began its attempt to dominate all of Europe by invading Poland, which prompted Great Britain and France to declare war on Germany. By the end of World War II in 1945, six million Jewish people had been murdered. The new German government outlawed Nazism and brought remaining Nazi officials to trial for the murders they'd committed.

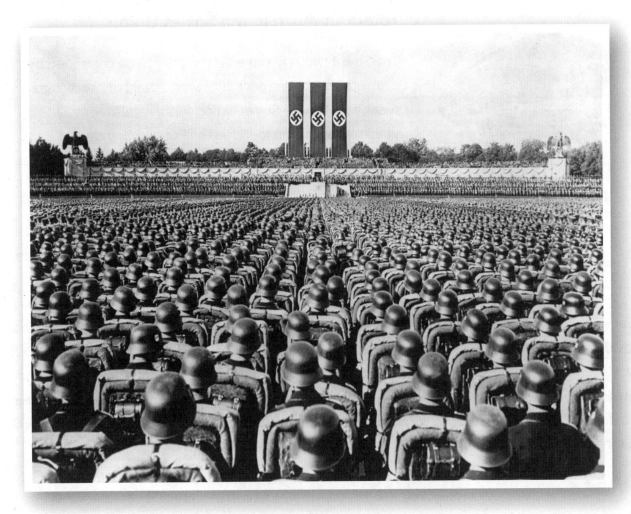

Spain Under Francisco Franco

The Spanish Civil War broke out in 1936, when nationalist rebels revolted against the democratically elected government. The rebels eventually seized control in 1939, with General Francisco Franco as their leader. Franco did not have any ideology that guided him but believed that military control was the only way to keep the country in order. Once in power, Franco put many officials of the previous Republican government to death. He banned all religions aside from Catholicism as well as the Catalan and Basque languages. Like Stalin, he created a secret police network that worked to arrest anyone who might oppose him. Franco also imposed strong censorship, hiring people to erase anything that was critical of him or Spain. Franco ruled until his death

in 1975, after which Spain held democratic elections. George Orwell fought for the Republicans in the Spanish Civil War, and it was in Spain that he first became concerned about the rise of totalitarianism.

Newspeak Words

Overview

In order to fully understand any story, the reader must understand the language spoken by its characters, and this includes the language of Newspeak in *1984*. This worksheet presents Newspeak words that students will encounter as they read the novel. Instruct students to look for these words as they read and to complete the chart by writing what they understand to be the definition of each word. Students should continue to complete this chart throughout the reading of *1984*.

Answer Key

Newspeak Word	Definition
doublethink	*the act of accepting multiple contradictory ideas at the same time*
thoughtcrime	*to think unorthodox thoughts*
blackwhite	*the willingness to say and know that black is white and to forget that one ever believed the contrary*
unperson	*someone who has been vaporized, or killed, by the government*
ownlife	*the subversive tendency to enjoy being individualistic*
facecrime	*a facial expression that suggests one is thinking unorthodox thoughts*
goodthinker	*someone who only has orthodox thoughts*
duckspeak	*to speak without thinking*
crimestop	*to prevent oneself from having unorthodox thoughts*

RL.11-12.4 Determine or clarify the meaning of unknown and multiple-meaning words and phrases based on grades 11–12 reading and content, choosing flexibly from a range of strategies.

Newspeak Words

Throughout *1984*, Orwell introduces words that are part of the language Newspeak, which aims to eliminate words that could be considered unorthodox.

Pay attention as these words are introduced in the novel, and, using your own words, complete the chart with each word's definition.

Newspeak Word	Definition
doublethink	*the act of accepting multiple contradictory ideas at the same time*
thoughtcrime	
blackwhite	
unperson	
ownlife	
facecrime	
goodthinker	
duckspeak	
crimestop	

Objective Summary Chart

Overview

Learning how to effectively summarize enables students to quickly get to the core of a story and focus on the more meaningful elements of a text. Students will use this worksheet to record the most important aspects of *1984* as they read. Pass out the worksheet before students begin reading the novel. Remind students to only list characters and events that are essential to understanding the story and to refrain from including any personal opinions about the characters, setting, and events. Once students' charts are completed, consider having students write a formal essay summarizing the novel.

Main Characters	*Winston Smith* *Julia* *Big Brother O'Brien*
Setting	*London, Oceania, in what is likely the year 1984*
Important Events	*Winston purchases illegal diary to write in.* *Julia slips Winston a note that says, "I love you," and they begin meeting in secret.* *Winston, O'Brien, and Julia meet about working against Big Brother.* *Soldiers seize Winston and Julia.* *O'Brien tortures and brainwashes Winston.* *Winston begs for Julia to be tortured, not him. Winston is released and loves Big Brother.*

RL.11-12.1 Cite strong and thorough textual evidence to support analysis of what the text says explicitly as well as inferences drawn from the text, including determining where the text leaves matters uncertain.

Objective Summary Chart

Complete this chart as you read *1984*, noting the main characters, the setting, and the most important events of the novel.

Main Characters	*Winston Smith*
Setting	
Important Events	*Winston purchases illegal diary to write in.*

The Dangers of Technology

Overview

Thoroughly exploring a single concept enables students to better understand a text's larger themes. Students will use this worksheet to answer questions about how technology can invade people's freedom and privacy as well as how the advancement of technology may seem dangerous to the Inner Party members.

RL.11-12.2 Determine two or more themes or central ideas of a text and analyze their development over the course of the text, including how they interact and build on one another to produce a complex account; provide an objective summary of the text.

The Dangers of Technology

When George Orwell wrote *1984* in 1949, technology was not nearly as advanced as it is today. However, he already saw the potential dangers technology posed to people's privacy and freedom.

Answer the following questions, thinking about how technology poses dangers to the citizens of Oceania as well as how Inner Party members fear the advancement of technology.

1. What are telescreens?

   A telescreen is a television that transmits video but also has a built-in camera and microphone. Telescreens are a requirement in everyone's home and all public spaces so that the Party can watch its members 24/7.

2. How does the author say the progression of technology from print to television helped the Party seize control?

3. Do Party members use technology to learn and explore new things?

4. Why are Party members concerned about the rise of automation?

5. Why do Party members want to stop the progression of technology?

Comparing Winston and Julia

Overview

Comparing and contrasting is a critical thinking skill essential to students' success both in and outside school. Students will use this worksheet to list the similarities and differences of the viewpoints of the two main characters in *1984*. Encourage students to fill out the chart as they learn new aspects of each character's personality or point of view.

RL.11-12.6 Analyze a case in which grasping a point of view requires distinguishing what is directly stated in a text from what is really meant (e.g., satire, sarcasm, irony, or understatement).

Comparing Winston and Julia

Winston Smith and Julia are the two most developed characters in *1984*. Although the action is told from Winston's point of view, he describes what he learns about Julia's point of view as they get to know one another.

Complete the chart by comparing and contrasting Winston's and Julia's opinions and viewpoints.

Winston's Opinions and Viewpoints	Julia's Opinions and Viewpoints	Shared Opinions and Viewpoints
Winston remembers life before the Party.	*Julia cannot imagine a world where the Party does not exist.*	*At the beginning of the novel, they hate Big Brother.*

Symbolism

Overview

Authors use symbols to represent major themes, provide information about a character or event, and add layers of meaning to a text. Students will use this worksheet to explore how Orwell uses various symbols in *1984* and how those symbols shape a central message of the novel. Ask students to pay attention to when these symbols are introduced and why they think Orwell included them. Have students answer the question at the bottom of the worksheet after they have finished the novel and completed the chart.

Answer Key

Sample Student Response

How do these symbols help you understand a central message of the novel?

Taken together, the telescreens and Big Brother convey how monitored and controlled everyone in Oceania is. Even within the novel, Winston believes Big Brother is a symbol and not an actual person. However, the Party acts as though the telescreens and Big Brother are a source of protection and not control. The proles and the paperweight symbolize that even though the Party wants its members to forget the past, there is still some evidence of how life used to be. The memory holes also symbolize how brazen the Party is in wanting people to forget any information that makes the Party look bad. Julia's sash and Goldstein are both reminders that there is opposition to the Party, both within it and outside it. These symbols all help convey the author's message that, as in all totalitarian societies, even though the Party has full control over Oceania, it still fears the memories and backlash of its people.

RL.11-12.3 Analyze the impact of the author's choices regarding how to develop and relate elements of a story or drama (e.g., where a story is set, how the action is ordered, how the characters are introduced and developed).

In literature, authors use symbols to represent different qualities or ideas without stating what they mean outright. For example, a beam of sunlight could symbolize hope, while a rain cloud could symbolize incoming danger.

Look for the symbols in this chart in *1984*. Explain the meaning of each symbol, and then answer the question about how these symbols shape the story.

Symbol	What It Means
the telescreens	*the sense of constant surveillance; no privacy*
Big Brother	
memory holes	
Julia's sash	
the proles	
the paperweight	
Goldstein	

How do these symbols help you understand a central message of the novel?

Descriptions of Settings

Overview

Authors carefully choose and describe a story's settings as each informs the story and its themes, reveals truths about events or characters, and creates the intended tone or mood of the work. Students will use this worksheet to explore this idea. Have students record the words the author uses to describe each place and then analyze what that description reveals about the story.

RL.11-12.5 Analyze how an author's choices concerning how to structure specific parts of a text (e.g., the choice of where to begin or end a story, the choice to provide a comedic or tragic resolution) contribute to its overall structure and meaning as well as its aesthetic impact.

Descriptions of Settings

Where a story is set and how the author describes that setting can tell readers a lot about a story and its themes. Pay attention to each new setting in *1984*. Record how the author describes each setting, and then write how that setting affects the story.

Setting	Description of Setting	What the Setting Tells You About the Story
Winston's apartment	*old, falling to pieces, dingy*	*Even Party members like Winston live in dreary, poor-quality buildings, meaning life for the people is not as good as the Party would have them believe.*
Ministry of Truth		
The countryside		
The room above Mr. Charrington's shop		
Ministry of Love		

*sparkteach   **37**

Driving Questions

Driving Questions	Initial Answer	Final Answer
How is Newspeak different from Oldspeak?	Text evidence:	Text evidence:
What changes with each new edition of the Newspeak dictionary?	Text evidence:	Text evidence:
What is the purpose in developing Newspeak?	Text evidence:	Text evidence:

Driving Questions	Initial Answer	Final Answer
How does Newspeak limit people's freedom?	Text evidence:	Text evidence:
What is the significance of calling Oceania's ruler "Big Brother"?	Text evidence:	Text evidence:
What contradictions exist in Newspeak?	Text evidence:	Text evidence:

Driving Questions	Initial Answer	Final Answer
Why can't citizens of Oceania learn other languages?	Text evidence:	Text evidence:
How does the party use Newspeak to control people's feelings and emotions?	Text evidence:	Text evidence:

Shades of Meaning

Word	Synonyms	Antonyms
good	*fine, excellent, wonderful, satisfactory, admirable*	*bad, terrible, disagreeable, deplorable, unpleasant*
freedom		
truth		
love		
exist		
orthodoxy		
thought		

Full Book Quiz

Overview

Use the following quiz to assess your students' comprehension and understanding of various plot elements and characters in *1984*. Note that in addition to the answer key that follows, answers can be found at SparkNotes.com/lit/1984/quiz. Ensure that students do not access the quiz and corresponding answers beforehand.

Answer Key

1. A	14. A
2. C	15. C
3. D	16. B
4. B	17. D
5. C	18. A
6. D	19. B
7. A	20. D
8. B	21. A
9. D	22. C
10. A	23. C
11. C	24. A
12. B	25. D
13. D	

1. How old is Julia?

   A. 26

   B. 30

   C. 32

   D. 35

2. Winston commits thoughtcrime by writing which of the following in his diary?

   A. I HATE BIG BROTHER

   B. DOWN WITH THE PARTY

   C. DOWN WITH BIG BROTHER

   D. DEATH TO BIG BROTHER

3. What piece of evidence of the Party's dishonesty does Winston remember having coming across several years earlier?

   A. A diary containing O'Brien's secret confession that Big Brother does not exist

   B. A videotape from a telescreen showing Inner Party members burning historical documents

   C. A tape-recorded conversation of Emmanuel Goldstein admitting that he is a Party operative, not a Party enemy

   D. A photograph proving that several individuals were out of the country when they were allegedly committing a crime

4. What organization urges children to turn their parents over to the authorities?

   A. The Party Youth

   B. The Junior Spies

   C. The Outer Party

   D. The Committee of Oceanian Patriotism

5. The psychological principle that allows an individual to believe contradictory ideas at the same time is called what?

    A. Doublemind

    B. Thoughtcrime

    C. Doublethink

    D. Doublespeak

6. Who really wrote the manifesto that O'Brien gives to Winston?

    A. Emmanuel Goldstein

    B. Big Brother

    C. Ayn Rand

    D. O'Brien

7. What does O'Brien use to torture Winston in Room 101?

    A. A cage full of rats

    B. A laser heat machine

    C. A machine that causes full-body physical pain

    D. Hallucinogenic drugs

8. Where do Winston and Julia make love for the first time?

    A. The room above the antiques shop

    B. The forest

    C. Trafalgar Square

    D. The beach

9. What is the last line of the St. Clement's Church song?

    A. Here comes the Party, dear Winston, you're dead!

    B. Here comes Big Brother to step on your shoe!

    C. Until the mousetrap goes snap! on your head!

    D. Here comes a chopper to chop off your head!

10. What does Winston trace in the dust on the table at the end of the novel?

    A. 2 + 2 = 5

    B. I love Big Brother

    C. I love Julia

    D. O'Brien

11. How many times does Julia claim to have had sex with Party members?

    A. 2

    B. 10

    C. Scores

    D. Hundreds

12. Which of the following characters is secretly a member of the Thought Police?

    A. Winston

    B. Mr. Charrington

    C. Syme

    D. Julia

13. What happens to the glass paperweight?

    A. It is confiscated by the Thought Police.

    B. Julia hides it under the mattress.

    C. O'Brien flings it out the window.

    D. It is shattered on the floor.

14. Where is the telescreen hidden in the room above Mr. Charrington's shop?

    A. Behind the picture of St. Clement's

    B. Under the bed

    C. Behind the light fixture

    D. Behind the poster of Big Brother

15. What is the name for the mass rally held every day?

    A. The Two Minutes Rage

    B. The Ten Minutes Hate

    C. The Two Minutes Hate

    D. The Daily Rage

16. Besides Oceania, what are the two countries that make up the rest of the Earth?

    A. Eurasia and Australasia

    B. Eurasia and Eastasia

    C. Eastasia and Africasia

    D. Australasia and Americom

17. What project is Syme working on at the beginning of the novel?

    A. A pamphlet on Emmanuel Goldstein

    B. A new slogan for the party

    C. A revision of a children's history book

    D. A Newspeak dictionary

18. Who turns Parsons in to the Thought Police?

    A. His children

    B. Julia

    C. His wife

    D. O'Brien

19. What does O'Brien say when Winston asks if he has been captured?

    A. "I would die before I would let that happen."

    B. "They got me a long time ago."

    C. "I'm afraid so."

    D. "I am one of them."

20. To what organization does Julia belong?

    A. The Junior Spies

    B. The Two Minutes Hate Committee

    C. The Inner Party

    D. The Junior Anti-Sex League

21. Winston has a memory of running away from his mother and sister and stealing what from them?

    A. Chocolate

    B. Clothing

    C. Money

    D. A diary

22. The setting for Winston's fantasy about Julia running toward him naked is

    A. Eastasia

    B. The Place Where There is No Darkness

    C. The Golden Country

    D. Ye Olde Curiosity Shoppe

23. In what nation did Orwell work for the British Imperial Police?

    A. Bangladesh

    B. Zanzibar

    C. Burma

    D. India

24. In what nation was Orwell born?

    A. India

    B. Bangladesh

    C. Zanzibar

    D. Burma

25. What was George Orwell's real name?

    A. Eric Snow

    B. Terrence Buskington

    C. Timothy Sneed

    D. Eric Blair

Section Quizzes

Overview

Use the following five-question quizzes to assess your students' comprehension of each section of *1984*. Note that in addition to the answer key that follows, answers can be found under "Further Study" at SparkNotes.com/lit/1984/. Ensure that students do not access the quizzes and corresponding answers beforehand.

Answer Key

Book One:
Chapter 1 Quick Quiz

1. B
2. C
3. A
4. A
5. D

Book One:
Chapters 2–3 Quick Quiz

1. D
2. C
3. C
4. C
5. D

Book One:
Chapters 4–6 Quick Quiz

1. A
2. B
3. A
4. D
5. A

Book One:
Chapters 7–8 Quick Quiz

1. C
2. A
3. A
4. C
5. C

Book Two:
Chapters 1–3 Quick Quiz

1. D
2. C
3. A
4. B
5. A

Book Two:
Chapters 4–6 Quick Quiz

1. C
2. D
3. B
4. C
5. B

Book Two:
Chapters 7–8 Quick Quiz

1. C
2. A
3. C
4. D
5. A

Book Two:
Chapters 9–10 Quick Quiz

1. C
2. B
3. C
4. A
5. C

Book Three:
Chapters 1–3 Quick Quiz

1. B
2. A
3. D
4. D
5. C

Book Three:
Chapters 4–6 Quick Quiz

1. C
2. A
3. D
4. C
5. A

Book One: Chapter 1 Quick Quiz

1. What can Winston's role in the Party best be described as?

    A. High-ranking

    B. Insignificant

    C. Undercover spy

    D. Informant

2. What is the purpose of the Ministry of Truth?

    A. To collect information about the Party's enemies

    B. To document historic events for future generations

    C. To alter historic records to fit the Party agenda

    D. To manage economic shortages in Oceania

3. What is the relationship between the proles and the Party?

    A. The Party considers the proles insignificant and nonthreatening.

    B. The Party considers the proles a population likely to rebel.

    C. The proles constitute the foundation of the national economy.

    D. The proles provide information to the Thought Police.

4. What leads Winston to believe O'Brien also hates the Party?

    A. Winston sees loathing in O'Brien's eyes before the Two Minutes Hate.

    B. O'Brien slips Winston a note that reveals his feelings toward the Party.

    C. A member of the revolution tells Winston about O'Brien.

    D. O'Brien flashes a symbol of the revolution to Winston.

5. What crime does Winston commit in Chapter 1?

    A. He visits a prole neighborhood.

    B. He skips a day of work.

    C. He is vocally critical of his superior.

    D. He starts a diary.

Book One: Chapters 2–3 Quick Quiz

1. Who comes to Winston's door while he is writing in his diary?

   A. Members of the Junior Spies

   B. The Thought Police

   C. O'Brien

   D. His neighbor, Mr. Parsons

2. What is the purpose of the Junior Spies?

   A. It is a television program that offers propaganda to Oceania's youth.

   B. It is a training program for future spies in the Oceania military.

   C. It trains children to spy on their parents and other adults.

   D. It teaches children to be ninjas.

3. What are the world's three ruling nations?

   A. America, Russia, and China

   B. America, Europe, and Asia

   C. Oceania, Eastasia, and Eurasia

   D. Oceania, Eastasia, and Westasia

4. Why does Winston have trouble remembering his childhood?

   A. He suffered a traumatic accident as a teenager.

   B. He has subconsciously buried the painful memories of his youth.

   C. He has no photos or other records of that time.

   D. He has been brainwashed by the Party.

5. When did Big Brother first emerge as a political figure?

   A. The 1930s

   B. The 1960s

   C. The 1950s

   D. It's unclear because the Party has altered historic documents.

Book One: Chapters 4–6 Quick Quiz

1. What is the public's reaction to the Party's efforts to alter historic records?

   A. For the most part, people accept the altered fact.

   B. People are left in a constant state of frustration.

   C. The Party's efforts breed contempt among the general population.

   D. The public never believes anything the Party says.

2. Who is Comrade Ogilvy?

   A. Winston's link to the rebellion

   B. A fictitious person invented by Winston

   C. A former Party official who has been vaporized

   D. A war hero who is being honored by the Party

3. What is the goal of Newspeak, as Syme explains it to Winston?

   A. To narrow language so that thoughtcrime is impossible

   B. To incorporate all languages into one

   C. To reduce the language to only pleasant-sounding words

   D. To make every word start with the letter *A*

4. What does Winston conclude the Party views sex as?

   A. A way to keep husbands and wives from cheating

   B. A way to keep the masses happy

   C. An outlet for stress and boredom

   D. A way to produce future Party members

5. TRUE or FALSE: Writing in his diary provides no relief for Winston's feelings of frustration and anger.

   A. True

   B. False

Book One: Chapters 7–8 Quick Quiz

1. Why won't the proles participate in a revolt against the Party?

   A. The Party treats them well.

   B. They figure they will be worse off in a revolution.

   C. They are ignorant of the Party's control over them.

   D. They believe that any revolt is destined to failure.

2. What Party lie does Winston uncover evidence of?

   A. They falsely accuse a former Party leader of treason.

   B. They falsely claimed that the Leader invented flight.

   C. They falsely claimed that they have won the war with Eastasia.

   D. They falsely claimed that 2 + 2 = 5.

3. Why does Winston consider suicide?

   A. He doesn't want to be captured and tortured by the Party.

   B. He hates his life.

   C. He can't face his true feelings for the dark-haired girl.

   D. He blames himself for his mother's death.

4. What is the Party motto?

   A. All for one and one for all.

   B. Tune in. Turn on. Drop out.

   C. War is peace. Freedom is slavery. Ignorance is strength.

   D. Big Brother is watching.

5. What does Winston buy at the secondhand store?

   A. A picture of a church

   B. A used book

   C. A glass paperweight

   D. An old history textbook

Book Two: Chapters 1–3 Quick Quiz

1. What is written on the note that the dark-haired girl passes to Winston?

    A. "O'Brien is a spy."

    B. "Big Brother is watching."

    C. "Meet me in the lunchroom."

    D. "I love you."

2. What effect does the dark-haired girl's note have on Winston?

    A. He hates her even more.

    B. He becomes worried that it is a setup.

    C. It reaffirms his will to live.

    D. It doesn't have much of an effect on him.

3. How does Winston react to the news that Julia has had sex with scores of Party members?

    A. He is thrilled that so many members of the Party are corrupt.

    B. He is disheartened that he was not her first.

    C. He feels used and betrayed.

    D. It makes no difference to him because he loves her.

4. Which statement best reflects Julia's views toward rebellion?

    A. Like Winston, she believes that rebellion will come from the proles.

    B. Unlike Winston she has no interest in rebellion.

    C. She believes that an awareness of sex will lead to mass rebellion within the Party.

    D. She believes that the Party is actually a good thing.

5. What does Winston tell Julia about his wife in Chapter 3?

    A. That he once thought about pushing her over a cliff

    B. That he truly loved her

    C. That he feels responsible for her death at the hands of the Party

    D. That they were never really married

Book Two: Chapters 4–6 Quick Quiz

1. What has prevented Julia and Winston from meeting more frequently?

   A. She has started to see another man.

   B. Winston's superiors at the ministry have become suspicious of his activities.

   C. They have been busy with preparations for Hate Week.

   D. Winston is unsure of his feelings toward Julia.

2. What is Winston's greatest fear?

   A. Being tortured by the Party

   B. That Julia will leave him

   C. Spiders

   D. Rats

3. What does Julia think of the Brotherhood?

   A. She feels their mission is doomed to failure.

   B. She thinks it is an invention of the Party.

   C. She wants to join but is afraid of being caught.

   D. She admires their cause.

4. What does O'Brien invite Winston to his house for?

   A. To read the secret handbook of the Brotherhood

   B. To meet with a leader in the rebellion

   C. To look at the new edition of the Newspeak dictionary

   D. To meet his wife and play poker with friends

5. What happens to Syme?

   A. He is killed in an explosion.

   B. He vanishes.

   C. He is promoted to Party manager.

   D. He is exposed as a spy.

Book Two: Chapters 7–8 Quick Quiz

1. What does Winston steal from his mother and sister the night they disappear?

    A. A book

    B. Their party credentials

    C. Chocolate

    D. Money

2. What do Winston and Julia decide is the wisest course of action to avoid being captured by the Party?

    A. Leave the room above Mr. Charrington's shop forever

    B. Get married

    C. Kill Mr. Charrington

    D. Commit suicide

3. What does O'Brien do that initially makes Winston feel safe in his apartment?

    A. O'Brien offers Winston a glass of wine.

    B. O'Brien kisses Winston on the cheek.

    C. O'Brien turns off the telescreen.

    D. O'Brien reveals that he has had sex with Julia.

4. What does O'Brien promise to give to Winston?

    A. A key to the Brotherhood's secret quarters

    B. Proof of the Party's lies

    C. A ticket out of the country

    D. The Brotherhood's manifesto

5. Where does Winston believe he will meet O'Brien again?

    A. In the place where there is no darkness

    B. In the afterlife

    C. In the secret headquarters of the Brotherhood

    D. In St. Clement's Church

Book Two: Chapters 9–10 Quick Quiz

1. How does the crowd react when the Party switches enemies from Eurasia to Eastasia?

    A. They riot because of the Party's deception.

    B. They ignore the change and continue to protest Eurasia.

    C. They are embarrassed and blame Goldstein for the mistake.

    D. They are disheartened and leave the rally.

2. According to the manifesto, why do the three global powers engage in perpetual war?

    A. Each country believes that it will eventually win control over the world.

    B. To keep the populace preoccupied and maintain power among the elite

    C. To encourage the development of better weaponry

    D. To consolidate economic power in the hands of the military

3. How does Julia react to what Winston reads from the manifesto?

    A. She is horrified and angered.

    B. She claims that it is false.

    C. She falls asleep.

    D. She begins to cry.

4. According to Winston and Julia, who might hold the key to the future?

    A. The red-armed prole

    B. Goldstein

    C. Others like them

    D. John Connor

5. Where in Winston and Julia's room was the telescreen hidden?

    A. In the glass paperweight

    B. Under the old wallpaper

    C. Behind the picture of St. Clement's Church

    D. In the ceiling

Book Three: Chapters 1–3 Quick Quiz

1. What is "the place where there is no darkness"?

    A. A courtroom

    B. A prison cell

    C. The mind

    D. An operating room

2. What happens to Winston to make him realize it's impossible for him to be a hero?

    A. His elbow is smashed in by a guard.

    B. He is bribed with money.

    C. The Party threatens to kill Julia.

    D. He is drugged.

3. What is doublespeak?

    A. Supporting the Party while knowing that it lies

    B. Speaking in two languages at once

    C. Betraying the Party

    D. Refusing to believe what you know is real

4. What causes Winston to weep in Chapter 3?

    A. He is told that Julia betrayed him.

    B. O'Brien explains that he will never escape.

    C. He finally realizes that he loves the Party.

    D. He sees his deteriorated face in a mirror.

5. Why does Winston feel gratitude toward O'Brien?

    A. O'Brien saves Winston from being shot.

    B. Winston feels this will bring O'Brien to end his torture.

    C. O'Brien acknowledges Winston's loyalty to Julia.

    D. O'Brien gives Winston a small portion of extra food.

Book Three: Chapters 4–6 Quick Quiz

1. What personal victory does Winston hope to achieve over the Party?

    A. He will convince them he is cured, then rise up in their ranks.

    B. He will kill O'Brien.

    C. He will die hating the Party, though they won't know it.

    D. He will refuse to eat and die of starvation.

2. What is in Room 101?

    A. The worst thing in the world

    B. An electric chair

    C. Julia

    D. Geometry

3. How does O'Brien know that Winston is finally "cured"?

    A. Winston professes his love for O'Brien.

    B. Winston promises to always love Big Brother.

    C. Winston denies his own existence.

    D. Winston betrays Julia.

4. What does Winston trace on the café table?

    A. Down with Big Brother

    B. Big Brother is watching

    C. 2 + 2 = 5

    D. Winston + Julia = 4eva

5. How does the image of Big Brother make Winston feel at the end of the novel?

    A. Safe and happy

    B. Proud

    C. Scared and paranoid

    D. Energetic and excited

Additional Quizzes

Overview

Use the following two quizzes to assess your students' comprehension of characters, themes, motifs, and symbols in *1984*. Note that in addition to the answer key that follows, answers can be found under "Further Study" at sparknotes.com/lit/1984. Ensure that students do not access the quizzes and corresponding answers beforehand.

Answer Key

Characters Quick Quiz

1. A
2. B
3. B
4. A
5. C

Themes, Motifs, and Symbols Quick Quiz

1. C
2. B
3. C
4. A
5. C

Characters Quick Quiz

1. What describes Julia's form of rebellion in comparison to Winston's?

   A. Small and personal

   B. Complete and uncompromising

   C. Strategic and well-planned

   D. Violent and aggressive

2. Who is the most dangerous man in Oceania?

   A. O'Brien

   B. Goldstein

   C. Winston

   D. Big Brother

3. What characteristics of O'Brien symbolize the Party?

   A. He is merciless and cruel.

   B. He is shadowy and enigmatic.

   C. He is both thoughtful and intelligent.

   D. He is masculine and hard-working.

4. What does Winston believe his relationship with Julia is?

   A. Temporary

   B. Codependent

   C. Superficial

   D. Innocent and pure

5. What does Winston's certainty that he will be captured by the Thought Police cause him to do?

   A. Destroy all traces of his thoughtcrimes

   B. Betray those around him

   C. Take increasingly risky actions in the name of rebellion

   D. Lead as normal a life as possible

Themes, Motifs, and Symbols Quick Quiz

1. What firsthand experiences did Orwell draw from when writing *1984*?

    A. Nazi Germany and fascist Italy

    B. The British subjugation of India

    C. The totalitarian regimes in Russia and Spain

    D. A life of poverty in France

2. What is the constant propaganda to which Oceania's citizens are subjected intended to do?

    A. Keep them calm and happy

    B. Disrupt their capacity for independent thought

    C. Encourage them to buy domestically made products

    D. Coax them toward nervous breakdown

3. What are the contradictory names of the various government ministries examples of?

    A. The control of information and history

    B. Totalitarianism

    C. Doublespeak

    D. Winston's attempts at rebellion

4. What does London's state of decay described in the novel indicate?

    A. The Party's lack of concern for the welfare of its citizens

    B. The common man's inability to care for himself

    C. A relatively low degree of technological advancement

    D. Economic collapse brought on by the Party's mismanagement

5. What is the importance of the red-armed woman?

    A. She saves Winston from the Thought Police.

    B. She is Winston's mother.

    C. She symbolizes hope for a future rebellion.

    D. She symbolizes Winston's sexual desire.

Writing Help—Suggested Essay Topics

Overview

Use the following four essay prompts to assess students' comprehension of characters, themes, and other key elements in *1984*.

Writing Help—Suggested Essay Topics

1. Describe Winston's character as it relates to his attitude toward the Party. In what ways might his fatalistic streak contribute to his ultimate downfall?

2. How does technology affect the Party's ability to control its citizens? In what ways does the Party employ technology throughout the book?

3. Discuss the idea of Room 101, the place where everyone meets his or her worst fear. Keeping in mind that for most of Winston's time at the Ministry of Love, he does not know what he will find in Room 101, what role does that uncertainty play in making Room 101 frightening? Does the cage of rats break Winston's spirit, or does it merely play a symbolic role?

4. What role does Big Brother play within the novel? What effect does he have on Winston? Is Winston's obsession with Big Brother fundamentally similar to or different from his obsession with O'Brien?

PART 4

Postmortem

After the unit, use the following Rubric for Student Assessment to assess your students' learning and the Student and Teacher Reflection worksheets to capture your experience with the Lesson Plans.

Rubric for Student Assessment

Overview

Using a rubric can help you assess students' learning more accurately and more consistently. Giving the rubric to your students before they begin a task that will be assessed also makes your expectations clear and encourages students to take responsibility for their own learning and success on an assignment. This rubric can be used across multiple midpoint activities and final projects to assess students' learning and understanding. You can also edit a version of the rubric to tailor it to specific learning goals you have for your classes.

Rubric for Student Assessment

Area of Performance	4	3	2	1
Content development	Work clearly and thoroughly addresses the prompt. All details/ideas support the main topic. Ideas are original, creative, and supported by numerous concrete details from the text.	Work mostly addresses the prompt. Most details/ideas support the main topic. A few concrete details from the text are provided.	Work doesn't stay on target and/or doesn't follow the prompt. Only a few supporting details are provided.	Work doesn't stay on target or follow the prompt. Ideas are confusing. Details are irrelevant or missing.
Organization	Details are presented in a logical and meaningful order. Essays or presentations include a clear introduction, body, and conclusion. Statements reflect critical thinking skills. Appropriate transitions are used to connect ideas.	Most details are presented in a logical order and are related to the main topic. The writing is clear, but the introduction, body, or conclusion needs strengthening.	Many details are presented in an illogical order or are unrelated to the main topic. The writing lacks a clear introduction, well-organized body, or a strong conclusion.	Details and ideas are poorly organized and unrelated to main topic.
Language and style	Writing or spoken language is smooth, coherent, and stays on topic. Sentence structure varies. Strong verbs and descriptive details and language clarify and strengthen ideas.	Writing or spoken language stays on topic but sentence structure doesn't vary. Some descriptive details are used to clarify ideas.	Some writing or spoken language doesn't flow and/or lacks creativity. Some language unrelated to or inappropriate for the main topic is used.	Writing or spoken language is confusing. Incomplete or run-on sentences are used. Many terms used are unrelated to or inappropriate for the main topic.

Area of Performance	4	3	2	1
Mechanics (when applicable)	All grammar and punctuation is correct. The writing is free of spelling errors.	The writing is mostly free of grammatical, mechanical, and spelling errors.	Writing contains several grammatical, punctuation, and spelling errors.	The writing contains numerous errors that make it difficult to understand.
Collaboration (when applicable)	Student played a valuable role in group work. Student worked well with others, listened respectfully to others' ideas, and resolved any challenges in an appropriate manner.	Student played an important role in group work but could have been more open to others' ideas and/or could have resolved challenges in a more constructive manner.	Student did minimal work in his/her group. Student ignored group challenges or left challenges unresolved.	Student didn't do her/his fair share of work. Student did not engage in the group task.
Research (when applicable)	Multiple, reliable sources were used to gather information. All sources are properly cited or credited.	Some research was done to complete the task. Not all sources are cited or some citations are incomplete.	Little or no research was done to gather necessary information. No sources are cited.	No research was done.

Student and Teacher Reflection Worksheets

Overview

A reflective practice helps you continue to develop new and engaging teaching strategies that meet the needs of all students in your class. Tracking successes as well as challenges throughout a unit of study also decreases planning time for future classes and helps you tailor your lessons to improve each time you teach them. Use this worksheet to reflect on a Real-Life Lens Lesson you have taught and record what was successful and what you would change when you teach the material again. Make notes on interesting ideas you added to the Lens Lesson or thoughts your students had that inspired you along the way.

Student Reflection Worksheet

1. How did reading the text through the lens of language as a form of control affect your engagement with and understanding of this text?

   _____

   _____

   _____

2. What difficulties did you encounter with this text, and how did you address them?

   _____

   _____

   _____

3. Consider the Real-Life Links you encountered at the beginning of the lesson. Which resources did you find the most interesting? Why?

   _____

   _____

4. How effective were the Driving Questions in guiding you to a deeper understanding of the text?

   _____

   _____

   _____

5. Describe one challenge you faced while working on an activity or project and how you overcame it.

   _____

   _____

   _____

6. What new insight or skill did you take away from this lesson?

   _____

   _____

   _____

Teacher Reflection Worksheet

1. How did the lens applied in this lesson affect student engagement and comprehension?

   _____

   _____

   _____

2. How did students respond to the Real-Life Links? Did some resources spark more interest than others?

   _____

   _____

   _____

3. Did you or any of your students come up with additional Driving Questions? If so, record them here to use the next time you teach this lesson.

   _____

   _____

4. Which activities inspired students the most?

   _____

   _____

   _____

5. What difficulties did students encounter, how did you address them, and were your interventions successful?

   _____

   _____

   _____

6. Were there worksheets, activities, or projects that you will revise the next time you present this lesson? If so, what changes will you make?

   _____

   _____

   _____

Notes

Notes

Notes

Notes

Notes